COMMUNICATION

WRITTEN BY DAVID LOWE

A READ-ABOUT

21

Communication is happening all around us. Every day we communicate.

We talk to each other, have conversations on the telephone, write letters, read newspapers, listen to the radio, and watch television.

All around us there are signs and symbols to tell us where we are, which way to go, what we should do, things to watch out for, and things we can buy.

We depend on our communication systems, and when they fail, it affects us and can cause us problems.

If a message is not delivered, if the television or telephone doesn't work, we feel annoyed.

If traffic lights fail or signs are missing, there can be accidents.

Communication is one of the most important things in our world.

Long ago, the very first people on earth could not talk. They made noises to communicate with each other. Later, these sounds developed into words.

Today, a baby learns how to speak in about two years. It learns to speak the language of its parents. In the world today, there are some 2,800 languages.

We use our language to communicate with each other.

For thousands of years people had to meet so that they could talk together.

Then in 1876, Alexander Graham Bell invented the telephone.

Telephones have changed the way we talk to each other. We can talk to anyone, anywhere in the world.

Today we have telephones in our homes, cars, boats, and even planes.

When people sent messages long ago, they were carried from place to place by runners or men on horseback.

The most famous messengers were the riders of the Pony Express, who carried letters right across the western United States.

A system of stamps and envelopes was developed in England. It was the beginning of our modern postal system.

Letters were first carried from place to place on mail coaches and later on ships, trains, trucks, and planes.

Today, every country has a postal service. Letters are delivered quickly anywhere in the world.

Modern technology has developed the fax machine. Now you can send a written message from one place to another as fast as you can speak.

Long ago, the town crier would stand in the marketplace and tell everyone the news of the day.

Wandering minstrels and storytellers would sometimes come to town and tell of great events in faraway places. People came from miles around.

Then with the invention of printing presses, newspapers became a good way of telling everyone the news.

When radio stations began to broadcast, people were able to listen to the news. Radio let us hear the voices of the people in the news.

Today, we can find out the news by reading newspapers, listening to radio, and watching television.

With the help of satellites, television can show us news events from everywhere in the world "live" as they happen.

People have been communicating for a long time by using signs and symbols to tell each other many different things.

Advertisements offer us things to buy. Signs give us information. They tell us what to do and where to find things. They help to keep us safe.

Many signs today have no words. They are picture signs that can be understood by all.

Symbols

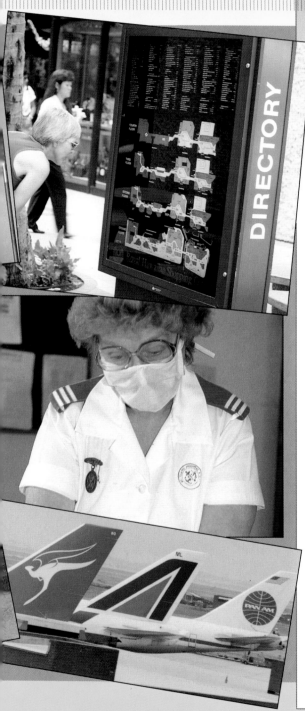

All around us there are symbols that tell us things about people and places.

Countries have flags, and most have a national dress for special occasions.

Some people wear special uniforms that tell us who they are or what job they do.

Companies also have their own special symbol or badge that tells us who they are.

Long ago, people found many ways to communicate with each other over long distances. They used sound and sight to warn each other of danger and to call for help. Today, we still use sound and sight signals to communicate.

Church bells, school bells, and alarm clocks tell us of special times. Warning bells, sirens, and flashing lights tell us of danger and help to keep us safe.

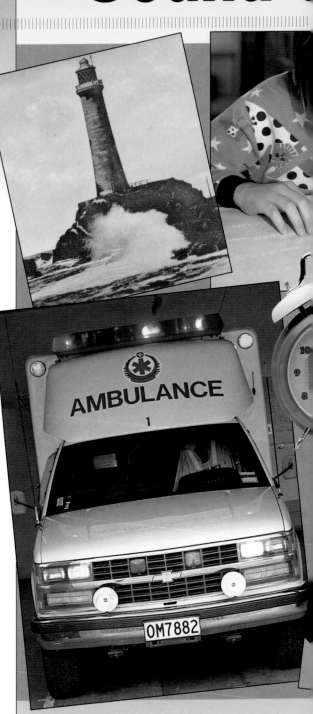

nd Sight

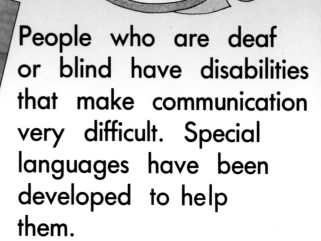

TO CROSS
STREET
PUSH
BUTTON
WAIT FOR
WALK
SIGNAL

People who are deaf or blind have disabilities that make communication very difficult. Special languages have been developed to help them.

People who are deaf are able to communicate by using their own sign language.

People who are blind are able to read and write by using a special raised-symbol language called Braille.

It is always hard to predict what will happen next. Technology in communication is growing rapidly and changing the way we live.

Computer systems will be used more and more. They could replace books, newspapers, and even the postal system.

Telephone callers may be able to see each other on a screen as they talk.

People, animals, and scenery will seem real when three-dimensional holograms are right in the middle of our living rooms.

Already there are machines that "talk" to one another. Maybe one day we will be communicating with thinking, talking robots.

No one can be sure what the future will be like, but it will be exciting.

Bibliography

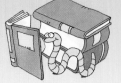

Books are a wonderful form of communication. Here are some more books to read that are all about using words and communication:

Codes and Messages
What Did You Say?
You Must Be Joking!
Playing with Words
Body Language
Animals Talk, Too
Names
A Pocket Full of Posies
Publishing a Book
Making a TV Series
Making a Record
Computers
Discovering the Past
Beyond 2000